MW01232499

Dedication

This First Book of Prayer is dedicated to

The Rev. Byron Tindall

The Rev. Ted Hackett

The Rev. Mary Johnson

Who so graciously contributed to this book to guide and provide inspirational understanding to Christians who worship, pray and strive to spread the Kingdom of God.

My First Book of Prayer
for Episcopal Children

By Arlene Krassa

Consultation and editing by Rev. Byron Tindall
Consultation and editing by Rev. Ted Hackett
Consultation and editing by Rev. Mary Johnson
Illustrations by Paula and Mark Krassa
Formatting by Mark Krassa

ISBN-10: 1-49056-413-6
ISBN-13: 978-1-49056-413-5

Table of Contents

My Special Prayers 7

Holy Baptism 16

The Holy Eucharist: Rite Two 33

The Holy Communion 44

Reconciliation of a Penitent 56

Psalms 59

Jesus Loves Us and Shows Us How to Show Our Love in Return 65

The Sermon on the Mount 68

Prayers and Thanksgivings 71

Liturgical Church Seasons..........................86

About Our Faith 93

Glossary 106

Dear Children,

      This is your own Book of Prayer for you to pray from at home and take to Church on Sunday. It will help you to praise God, to thank him, and love him.

      You will find pictures and prayers that will help you to pray with the Celebrant and your Church family. The words that are in heavy black are to be said aloud.

      To grow to be more like Jesus, we love God with all our heart, all our soul and our entire mind, and love our neighbors as ourselves. To help us to do this we talk to God with our prayers; listen for him to speak to us, and ask him to help us.

My Special Prayers

The apostles asked Jesus to teach them to pray,
Jesus gave them this special prayer:
Luke 11:1–4

The Lord's Prayer

Our Father,
who art in heaven,
hallowed be thy name.
your kingdom come,
your will be done,
on earth as it is in heaven.
Give us this day our daily bread.
forgive us our sins,
as we forgive those who sin against us.
Save us from the time of trial,
and deliver us from evil.

For the kingdom, the power,
and the glory are yours,
now and forever. *Amen.*

Apostles' Creed

I believe in God, the Father almighty,
creator of heaven and earth;
I believe in Jesus Christ, his only Son, our Lord.
He was conceived by the power of the Holy Spirit
and born of the Virgin Mary.
He suffered under Pontius Pilate,
was crucified, died, and was buried.
He descended to the dead.
On the third day he rose again.
He ascended into heaven,
and is seated at the right hand of the Father.
He will come again to judge the living and the
dead.
I believe in the Holy Spirit,
the holy catholic Church,
the communion of saints,
the forgiveness of sins
the resurrection of the body,
and the life everlasting. Amen.

Glory to the Father

Glory to the Father,
and to the Son,
and to the Holy Spirit,
as it was in the beginning,
is now, and will be forever.
Amen.

Morning Prayers

Lord God, almighty and everlasting Father, you
have brought us in safety to this new day: Preserve
us with your mighty power, that we may not fall
into sin, nor be overcome by adversity; and in all
we do, direct us to the fulfilling of your purpose;
through Jesus Christ our Lord.
Amen.

Open my lips, O lord,
  and my mouth shall proclaim your praise
Create in me a clean heart, O God,
  and renew a right spirit within me.
Cast me not away from your presence
  and take not your Holy Spirit from me.
Give me the joy of your saving help again
  and sustain me with your bountiful Spirit.

Glory to the Father, and to the Son, and to the Holy Spirit:
as it was in the beginning is now, and will be forever.
Amen.

Glory to God
Gloria in excelsis

Glory to God in the highest,
and peace to his people on earth.
Lord God, heavenly king,
almighty God and Father,
We worship you, we give you thanks,
we praise you for your glory.
Lord Jesus Christ, only Son of the Father,
Lord God, Lamb of God,
you take away the sin of the world:
have mercy on us;
you are seated at the right hand of the Father:
receive our prayer.
For you alone are the Holy One,
you alone are the Lord,
you alone are the Most High,
Jesus Christ,
with the Holy Spirit,
in the glory of God the Father. *Amen.*

For Joy of God's Creation

O heavenly Father,
you have filled the world with beauty:
Open my eyes to behold your gracious hand
 in all your works, that, rejoicing in your whole
creation,
 I may learn to serve you with gladness;
 for the sake of him through whom all
things were made, your Son Jesus Christ our Lord.
Amen.

A Prayer by St. Francis

Lord, make us an instrument of your peace.
Where there is hatred, let us sow love;
where there is injury, pardon;
where there is discord, union;

where there is doubt, faith; where there is despair, hope;
where there is darkness, light;
where there is sadness, joy.
Grant that we may not so much
seek to be consoled as to console;
to be understood as to understand;
to be loved as to love.
For it is in giving that we receive;
it is in pardoning that we are pardoned;
and it is in dying that we are born to eternal life.

Evening Prayers

O gracious Light,
pure brightness of the ever living Father in heaven,
O Jesus Christ, Holy and blessed!
Now as we come to the setting of the sun,
and our eyes behold the vesper light,
we sing your praises O God; Father Son, and Holy Spirit.

You are worthy at all times to be praised by happy voices,
O Son of God, O Giver of life,
and to be glorified through all the worlds.
Amen.

O God, we thank you for having kept us safe today and for having given us so many blessings and graces.
Please bless our family
and all who love and care for us.
we renew our faith to you
and ask your forgiveness for all our sins.
Bless this night that it may be filled with your peace. *Amen*

Dear Lord Jesus

Dear Lord Jesus, please watch over and protect our family in this ever changing world: Show us that your ways give more life than the ways of the world, and that following you is better than chasing after selfish goals. Please help us to take failure and learn from it to do better. Give us strength to keep our faith in you. Help us to love each other and treasure each and every family moment you have blessed us with; through Jesus Christ Our Lord.
Amen

Prayers for Meals

Bless us O Lord with these thy gifts
which we are about to receive from your
bounty through Christ our Lord.
Amen.

Dear Lord, thank you for this food.
Bless the hands that prepared it.
Bless it to our use and to your service.
And make us ever mindful of the needs of others.
Through Christ our Lord we pray.
Amen.

Our Church is where we gather together on Sundays as a community to worship God. We celebrate the two greatest Sacraments of Holy Baptism and Holy Communion as a Church family. Our priest generally leads the Church service. The priest uses the Bible and grace by God to give us lessons and blessings.

Baptism is the service we use to make people, generally infants and young children, members of our Church family.

When a person is to be baptized, we all renew our Baptismal vows together with a special service. We then welcome the newly baptized person or persons into our Church community.

In the pages that follow are a Holy Baptism service and a version of the Holy Eucharist service. These were written for you to follow along with your priest and Church family.

Holy Baptism

A hymn, psalm, or anthem may be sung.

The people standing, the Celebrant says

> Blessed be God: Father, Son, and Holy Spirit.

People **And blessed be his kingdom, now and forever. Amen.**

The Celebrant then continues

> There is one Body and one Spirit;

People **There is one hope in God's call to us;**

Celebrant	One Lord, one Faith, one Baptism;
People	**One God and Father of all.**

Celebrant	The Lord be with you.
People	**And also with you.**
Celebrant	Let us pray.

The Collect of the Day

The Celebrant says the Collect.

> *[A collect is a prayer that "collects" the
> thoughts of all of the people gathered to
> worship, focuses those thoughts on one
> special truth about God, and asks God's
> blessing on those who pray. The collect goes
> with the special day or season we are
> observing]*

People:　　**Amen**

The Lessons

The people sit. One or two Lessons, as appointed, are read, the Reader first saying

A Reading (Lesson) from_____.

A citation giving chapter and verse may be added.

After each Reading, the Reader may say

The Word of the Lord.
People **Thanks be to God.**

Or the Reader may say

Here ends the Reading (Epistle).

Silence may follow.

A Psalm, hymn, or anthem may follow each Reading.

Then, all standing, the Deacon or a Priest reads the Gospel, first saying

The Holy Gospel of Our Lord Jesus Christ according to_____.
People **Glory to you, Lord Christ.**

After the Gospel, the Reader says

The Gospel of the Lord.
People   **Praise to you, Lord Christ.**

The Sermon

The Sermon may be preached before or after the Peace.

Presentation and Examination of the Candidates

The Celebrant says

The Candidate(s) for Holy Baptism will now be presented.

Adults and Older Children

The candidates who are able to answer for themselves are presented individually by their Sponsors, as follows

Sponsor   I present *N*. to receive the
              Sacrament of Baptism.

The Celebrant asks each candidate when presented
              Do you desire to be baptized?

Candidate   I do.

Infants and Younger Children

Candidates who are unable to answer for themselves are presented individually by their Parents and Godparents, as follows

Parents and Godparents
> I present *N.* to receive the Sacrament of Baptism.

When all have been presented the Celebrant asks the parents and godparents the following:
> Will you be responsible for seeing that the child you present is brought up in the Christian faith and life?

Parents and Godparents
> I will, with God's help.

Celebrant
> Will you by your prayers and witness help this child to grow into the full stature of Christ?

Parents and Godparents
> I will, with God's help.

Then the Celebrant asks the following questions of the candidates who can speak for themselves and of the parents and godparents who speak on behalf of the infants and younger children.

Question	Do you renounce Satan and all the spiritual forces of wickedness that rebel against God?
Answer	I renounce them.
Question	Do you renounce the evil powers of this world which corrupt and destroy the creatures of God?
Answer	I renounce them.
Question	Do you renounce all sinful desires that draw you from the love of God?
Answer	I renounce them.
Question	Do you turn to Jesus Christ and accept him as your Savior?
Answer	I do.
Question	Do you put your whole trust in his grace and love?
Answer	I do.
Question	Do you promise to follow and obey him as your Lord?
Answer	I do.

After all have been presented, the Celebrant addresses the congregation, saying
>Will you who witness these vows do all in your power to support *these persons* in *their* life in Christ?

People **We will.**

The Celebrant then says these or similar words
>Let us join with *those* who are committing *themselves* to Christ and renew our own baptismal covenant.

The Baptismal Covenant

Celebrant Do you believe in God the Father?
People **I believe in God, the Father almighty, creator of heaven and earth.**
Celebrant Do you believe in Jesus Christ, the Son of God?
People **I believe in Jesus Christ, his only Son, our Lord.
He was conceived by the power of the Holy Spirit and born of the Virgin Mary.**

23

He suffered under Pontius
Pilate, was crucified, died, and
was buried.
He descended to the dead.
On the third day he rose again.
He ascended into heaven,
and is seated at the right hand of
the Father.
He will come again to judge the
living and the dead.

Celebrant Do you believe in God the Holy
Spirit?

People **I believe in the Holy Spirit,
the holy Catholic Church,
the communion of saints,
the forgiveness of sins,
the resurrection of the body,
and the life everlasting.**

Celebrant Will you continue in the apostles'
teaching and fellowship, in the
breaking of bread, and in the
prayers?

People **I will, with God's help.**

Celebrant Will you persevere in resisting evil,
and, whenever you fall into sin,
repent and return to the Lord?

People **I will, with God's help.**

Celebrant	Will you proclaim by word and example the Good News of God in Christ?
People	**I will, with God's help.**
Celebrant	Will you seek and serve Christ in all persons, loving your neighbor as yourself?
People	**I will, with God's help.**
Celebrant	Will you strive for justice and peace among all people, and respect the dignity of every human being?
People	**I will, with God's help.**

Prayers for the Candidates

The Celebrant then says to the congregation

Let us now pray for *these persons* who *are* to receive the sacrament of new birth [and for those (this person) who *have* renewed *their* commitment to Christ.]

A Person appointed leads the following petitions

Leader	Deliver *them,* O Lord, from the way of sin and death.
People	**Lord, hear our prayer.**

Leader	Open *their hearts* to your grace and truth.
People	**Lord, hear our prayer.**
Leader	Fill *them* with your holy and life–giving Spirit.
People	**Lord, hear our prayer.**
Leader	Keep *them* in the faith and communion of your holy Church.
People	**Lord, hear our prayer.**
Leader	Teach *them* to love others in the power of the Spirit.
People	**Lord, hear our prayer.**
Leader	Send *them* into the world in witness to your love.
People	**Lord, hear our prayer.**
Leader	Bring *them* to the fullness of your peace and glory.
People	**Lord, hear our prayer.**

The Celebrant says

Grant, O Lord, that all who are baptized into the death of Jesus Christ your Son may live in the power of his resurrection and look for him to come again in glory; who lives and reigns now and forever. *Amen.*

Thanksgiving over the Water

The Celebrant blesses the water, first saying

The Lord be with you.

People	**And also with you.**
Celebrant	Let us give thanks to the Lord our God.
People	**It is right to give him thanks and praise.**

Celebrant

We thank you, Almighty God, for the gift of water. Over it the Holy Spirit moved in the beginning of creation. Through it you led the children of Israel out of their bondage in Egypt into the land of promise. In it your Son Jesus received the baptism of John and was anointed by the Holy Spirit as the Messiah, the Christ, to lead us, through his death and resurrection, from the bondage of sin into everlasting life.

We thank you, Father, for the water of Baptism. In it we are buried with Christ in his death. By it we share in his resurrection. Through it we are reborn by the Holy Spirit. Therefore, in joyful obedience to your Son, we bring into his fellowship those who come to him in faith, baptizing them in the Name of the Father, and of the Son, and of the Holy Spirit.

At the following words, the Celebrant touches the water

Now sanctify this water, we pray you, by the power of your Holy Spirit, that those who here are cleansed from sin and born again may continue forever in the risen life of Jesus Christ our Savior.

To him, to you, and to the Holy Spirit, be all honor and glory, now and forever. ***Amen.***

The Baptism

Each candidate is presented by name to the Celebrant, or to the assisting priest or deacon, who then immerses, or pours water upon, the candidate, saying:

N., I baptize you in the Name of the Father, and of the Son,and of the Holy Spirit. **Amen.**

When this action has been completed for all candidates, the Bishop or Priest, at a place in full sight of the congregation, prays over them, saying

Let us pray.

Heavenly Father, we thank you that by water and the Holy Spirit you have bestowed upon *these* your servants the forgiveness of sin, and have raised *them* to the new life of grace. Sustain *them,* O Lord, in your Holy Spirit. Give *them* an inquiring and discerning heart, the courage to will and to persevere, a spirit to know and to love you, and the gift of joy and wonder in all your works. *Amen.*

Then the Bishop or Priest places a hand on the person's head, marking on the forehead the sign of the cross [using Chrism if desired] and saying to each one

N., you are sealed by the Holy Spirit in Baptism and marked as Christ's own forever. **Amen.**

This action may also be done immediately after the administration of the water and before the preceding prayer.

When all have been baptized, the Celebrant says

Let us welcome the newly baptized.

Celebrant and People

We receive you into the household of God. Confess the faith of Christ crucified, proclaim his resurrection, and share with us in his eternal priesthood.

If Confirmation, Reception, or the Reaffirmation of Baptismal Vows is not to follow, the Peace is now exchanged.

| Celebrant | The peace of the Lord be always with you. |
| People | **And also with you.** |

At the Eucharist

[The service will then continue with Prayers of the People or Offertory of the Eucharist.]

Alternative Ending

[If there is no celebration of the Eucharist, the service will continue with the Lord's Prayer. After the Lord's Prayer, the service will continue as follows.]

The Celebrant then says

All praise and thanks to you, most merciful Father, for adopting us as your own children, for incorporating us into your holy Church, and for making us worthy to share in the inheritance of the saints in light; through Jesus Christ your Son our Lord, who lives and reigns with you and the Holy Spirit, one God, for ever and ever. *Amen.*

[Alms may be received and presented at this time. Other prayers may also be added, ending with the following prayer.]

Almighty God, the Father of our Lord Jesus Christ, from whom every family in heaven and earth is named, grant you to be strengthened with might by his Holy Spirit, that, Christ dwelling in your hearts by faith, you may be filled with all the fullness of God. *Amen.*

The Holy Eucharist: Rite Two

Entrance Hymn

[We all stand and sing a hymn as the Verger, (sometimes the Thurifer, carries the smoking incense) Crucifer, Torch Bearers, Deacon and Priest process to the altar. On occasion the Choir joins the procession.]

The Word of God

Celebrant   Blessed be God: Father, Son, and Holy Spirit.

People   **And blessed be his kingdom, now and forever. Amen.**

The Celebrant may say
Almighty God, to you all hearts are open, all desires known, and from you no secrets are hid: Cleanse the thoughts of our hearts by the inspiration of your Holy Spirit that we may perfectly love you, and worthily magnify your holy name; through Christ our Lord.

People   **Amen.**

Sometimes, we stand and sing or say:

Glory to God in the highest,
and peace to his people on earth.

Lord God, heavenly king,
almighty God and Father,
we worship you, we give you thanks,
we praise you for your glory.

Lord Jesus Christ, only Son of the Father,
Lord God, Lamb of God,
you take away the sin of the world:
have mercy on us;
you are seated at the right hand of the Father:
receive our prayer.

For you alone are the Holy One,
you alone are the Lord,
you alone are the Most High,
Jesus Christ.
with the Holy Spirit,
in the glory of God the Father. Amen.

[On other occasions the following is used]

Lord, have mercy. Kyrie eleison.
Christ, have mercy. or Christe eleison
Lord have mercy.   Kyrie eleison.
or this
Holy God,
Holy and Mighty
Holy Immortal One,
Have mercy upon us

The Collect of the Day

Celebrant   The Lord be with you.

People   **And also with you.**

Celebrant   Let us pray.

The Celebrant says the Collect.
[A collect is a prayer that "collects" the thoughts of
all of the people gathered to worship, focuses those
thoughts on one special truth about God, and asks
God's blessing on those who pray. The collect goes
with the special day or season we are observing]

People: **Amen.**

[We recall the following Bible Scriptures in our minds and hearts as we celebrate the Sacrament of Holy Communion.]

Exodus 12:1–8
John 2:1–11
Luke 9:10–17
Luke 22:17–20

The Lessons

The people sit. *[We stand to praise God, we sit to hear and think about God's Word, and we kneel to pray or adore God.]*

We listen to one or two readings from the Bible.

After each reading, the Reader may say

Reader   The Word of the Lord.

People   **Thanks be to God.**

[Sometimes, we all stand and sing a hymn as the Celebrant or Deacon, Crucifer and Torch Bearers process to the center of the Church for the Gospel reading. In some Churches, the Gospel is read from the pulpit or lectern.

On Sunday the Priest or Deacon reads a gospel lesson from the Bible that will teach you something that Jesus said or did when he was on earth.

When the Gospel is read from the center of the Church, it is because the Good News of the Gospel is for the people. So, as a sign that Jesus is with us when we gather to worship him, the Celebrant or Deacon reads the Gospel while standing among the people.]

Celebrant or Deacon reads the Gospel, first saying

The Holy Gospel of our Lord Jesus Christ

People   **Glory to you, Lord Christ.**

After the Gospel, the reader says:
                    The Gospel of the Lord

People   **Praise to you, Lord Christ**

The Sermon

The Priest or Deacon asks us to sit.

[We sit quietly and listen carefully to the preacher, who shows us how the words of the Bible help us understand God's plan for our lives. After the Sermon, we pray for a moment in silence.]

The Nicene Creed

[Christians have been saying this summary of what we, as a Church, believed about God for more than 1500 years. When we say the Nicene Creed, we are saying what we believe, and we are aware of all the

followers of Jesus who have lived in earlier times and
are now with God.]

All stand and say together
We believe in one God,
the Father, the Almighty,
maker of heaven and earth,
of all that is, seen and unseen.

We believe in one Lord, Jesus Christ,
the only Son of God,
eternally begotten of the Father,
God from God, Light from Light,
true God from true God,
begotten, not made,
of one Being with the Father.
Through him all things were made.
For us and for our salvation
he came down from heaven:
by the power of the Holy Spirit
he became incarnate from the Virgin Mary,
and was made man.
For our sake he was crucified under Pontius
Pilate;
he suffered death and was buried.
On the third day he rose again
in accordance with the Scriptures;

he ascended into heaven
and is seated at the right hand of the Father.
He will come again in glory to judge the living
and the dead,
and his kingdom will have no end.

We believe in the Holy Spirit, the Lord, the giver
of life,
who proceeds from the Father and the Son.
With the Father and the Son he is worshiped and
glorified.
He has spoken through the Prophets.
We believe in one holy catholic and apostolic
Church.
We acknowledge one baptism for the
forgiveness of sins.
We look for the resurrection of the dead,
and the life of the world to come. Amen.

The Prayers of the People

*At this time, we kneel or stand to ask God's help or
blessing for:*

The Universal Church, its members, and its mission
The Nation and all in authority
The welfare of the world

The concerns of the local community
Those who suffer and those in any trouble
Those who have died.

[There are different forms that may be used.
Sometimes the leader, Celebrant or Deacon will ask
the people to repeat a response, such as "Lord, have
mercy," or "Hear our prayer." Often there will be a
special time for you to say out loud the names of
those you are praying for, or to thank God for a
special blessing.]

When the prayers are concluded the Celebrant adds
a concluding collect.

Confession of Sin

We usually kneel to confess our sins.

The Deacon or Celebrant says

Let us confess our sins against God and our
neighbor.

All people now say together
Most merciful God,
we confess that we have sinned against you

in thought, word, and deed,
by what we have done,
and by what we have left undone.
We have not loved you with our whole heart;
we have not loved our neighbors as ourselves.
We are truly sorry and we humbly repent.
For the sake of your Son Jesus Christ,
have mercy on us and forgive us;
that we may delight in your will,
and walk in your ways,
to the glory of your Name. Amen.

The Priest stands and says to the people

Almighty God have mercy on you, forgive you all your sins through our Lord Jesus Christ, strengthen you in all goodness, and by the power of the Holy Spirit keep you in eternal life. **Amen.**

The Peace

All stand.

The Celebrant says to the people

> The peace of the Lord be
> always with you.

People   **And also with you.**

*[At this time the Ministers and people greet one
another in the name of the Lord. We often offer one
another a hand, or a hug, and say one of the
following.]*

The peace of the Lord
or
Peace be with you.

The Holy Communion

Celebrant may begin the Offertory by saying
I appeal to you, my brothers and sisters, by the mercies of God, that you present yourselves in living sacrifice.

[During the Offertory, a hymn, psalm, or anthem may be sung. If the choir sings, try to listen not only to the words, but also to the mood that the music tries to convey. The choir is not performing, and we who listen are not an audience. We are all worshiping together.]

Members of the congregation bring the people's offerings of bread and wine, and money or other gifts, to the celebrant. The people stand while the offerings are presented and placed on the Altar.

[The people sit as the Deacon or Celebrant place the gifts upon the Altar. All stand and sing an offertory Hymn. There are many hymns that may be sung; this is one.]

Praise God from whom all blessings flow
Praise him, all creatures here below.
Praise him above, ye heavenly hosts!
Praise Father, Son, and Holy Ghost.

The Great Thanksgiving

[There are different Eucharistic prayers, which may be used. Eucharistic Prayer A is the one that follows. Whichever prayer is used, we listen and respond as called upon.]

Eucharistic Prayer A

The people stand.
The Celebrant faces the people and sings or says

The Lord be with you.

People	**And also with you.**
Celebrant	Lift up your hearts.
People	**We lift them to the Lord.**
Celebrant	Let us give thanks to the Lord our God.
People	**It is right to give him thanks and praise.**

Then, facing the Holy Table, the Celebrant says

It is right, and a good and joyful thing, always and everywhere to give thanks to you, Father Almighty, creator of heaven and earth.

[The celebrant continues with a special reason for giving thanks, which changes as we move through the seasons of the Church Year, and then says:]

Therefore we praise you, joining our voices with Angels and Archangels and with all the company of heaven, who forever sing this hymn to proclaim the glory of your Name.

Celebrant and People sing or say

**Holy, holy, holy Lord, God of power and might heaven and earth are full of your glory.
Hosanna in the highest.
Blessed is he who comes in the name of the Lord.
Hosanna in the highest.**

The people stand or kneel.

The Celebrant continues

Holy and gracious Father: In your infinite love you made us for yourself, and, when we had fallen into sin and become subject to evil and death, you, in your mercy, sent Jesus Christ, your only and eternal Son, to share our human nature, to live and die as one of us, to reconcile us to you, the God and Father of all. He stretched out his arms upon the cross, and offered himself, in obedience to your will, a perfect sacrifice for the whole world.

[At this part of the Great Thanksgiving during this prayer, in a mysterious way no one fully understands, the bread and wine become the Body and Blood of Jesus. The Celebrant holds up or lays hands upon them and says the words that follow.]

The celebrant continues

On the night he was handed over to suffering and death, our Lord Jesus Christ took bread; and when he had given thanks to you, he broke it, and gave it to his disciples, and said, "Take, eat: This is my Body, which is given for you. Do this for the remembrance of me."

After supper he took the cup of wine; and when he had given thanks, he gave it to them, and said, "Drink this, all of you: This is my Blood of the new Covenant, which is shed for you and for many for the forgiveness of sins. Whenever you drink it, do this for the remembrance of me."
Therefore we proclaim the mystery of faith:

Celebrant and people say

Christ has died.
Christ is risen.
Christ will come again.

The celebrant continues

We celebrate the memorial of our redemption, O Father, in this sacrifice of praise and thanksgiving. Recalling his death, resurrection, and ascension, we offer you these gifts.

Sanctify them by your Holy Spirit to be for your people the Body and Blood of your Son, the holy food and drink of new and unending life in him. Sanctify us also that we may faithfully receive this holy sacrament, and serve you in unity, constancy, and peace; and at the last day bring us with all your saints into the joy of your eternal kingdom.

All this we ask through your Son Jesus Christ: By him, and with him, and in him, in the unity of the Holy Spirit all honor and glory is yours, Almighty Father, now and for ever. **Amen.**

The Celebrant says

And now, as our Savior
Christ has taught us,
we are bold to say,

Celebrant and people say

Our Father, who art in heaven,
Hollowed be thy Name,
thy kingdom come,
thy will be done,
on earth as it is in heaven.
Give us this day our daily bread.
And forgive us our trespasses,
as we forgive those
who trespass against us.
And lead us not into temptation,
but deliver us from evil.
For thine is the kingdom,
and the power, and the glory,
for ever and ever. *Amen.*

[The Celebrant and people may say the traditional version of our Lord's Prayer as seen previously, or they may say the contemporary version as seen on the following page.]

Our Father in heaven,
hallowed be your Name,
your kingdom come,
your will be done,
on earth as in heaven.
Give us today our daily bread.
Forgive us our sins
as we forgive those
who sin against us.
Save us from the time of trial,
and deliver us from evil.
For the kingdom, the power,
and the glory are yours,
now and forever. ***Amen.***

The Breaking of the Bread

The Celebrant breaks the consecrated Bread.

There is a period of silence.

Celebrant says
Christ our Passover is sacrificed for us;

Celebrant and people
Therefore let us keep the feast.

The Celebrant faces the people and says the following invitation
The gifts of God for the People of God.

The ministers receive the Sacrament in both kinds, and then deliver it to the people.

[In larger Churches, the ushers then stand by each Church pew one at a time to show the people it is time to go up to the altar to receive the Body and Blood of Christ.

When you kneel at the altar rail to receive communion, put your right hand, palm up, over your left hand. You may sip from the chalice as it is offered to you, or you may prefer to dip the host in the cup and receive the Blood of Christ in this way.]

The Bread and Cup are given to the people with these words:

The Body of Christ, the bread of heaven. **Amen.**

The Blood of Christ, the cup of salvation. **Amen.**

During Holy Communion, hymns, psalms, or anthems may be sung. Listen to this music, sing the hymns, or use this quiet time to pray.

After Communion, the Celebrant says
Let us pray.

Celebrant and people say

**Eternal God, heavenly Father,
you have graciously accepted us as living members
of your Son our Savior Jesus Christ,
and you have fed us with spiritual food
in the Sacrament of his Body and Blood.
Send us now into the world in peace,
and grant us strength and courage
to love and serve you
with gladness and singleness of heart;
through Christ our Lord. Amen.**

The Priest then gives the people a blessing.

[The Bishop or Priest asks God to bless his people using a form suitable to the season or a blessing that can be used at any time of the year. An example is below.]

May the Peace of God which passes all understanding keep your hearts and minds in the knowledge and love of God and His Son Jesus Christ our Lord, and may the blessing of God Almighty, Father, Son and Holy Spirit, rest upon you now and ever more.

The Dismissal

[We all stand and sing a hymn as the Crucifer, Torch Bearers, Priest and Deacon Process from the altar to the doorway of the Church.]

[After the hymn the Deacon or Priest says these words from the back of the Church, sending us into the world with the love of Christ to serve people in his name.]

Deacon or Priest says:
Go in peace to love and serve the Lord.

People say   **Thanks be to God**

Reconciliation of a Penitent

While private confession of sins is not a requirement, anyone may request the reconciliation of a penitent from a priest and receive assurance of God's forgiveness. The confession is always made in private and kept in strict confidence.

[This means that the priest will not ever tell anyone what you have told him or her.]

A confession can be heard anytime and anywhere. After a confession is heard the priest may counsel the penitent on his or her sins, then, may assign a prayer, psalm or hymn, or something to be done as a sign of penitence and act of thanksgiving. There are two forms that can be used for a confession. Form One is below.]

Form One

The Penitent begins.

Bless me, for I have sinned.

The Priest says

The Lord be in your heart and upon your lips that you may truly and humbly confess your sins: In the Name of the Father, and of the Son, and of the Holy Spirit. *Amen.*

Penitent

I confess to Almighty God, to his Church, and to you, that I have sinned by my own fault in thought, word, and deed, in things done and left undone; especially _____. For these and all other sins which I cannot now remember, I am truly sorry. I pray God to have mercy on me. I firmly intend amendment of life, and I humbly beg forgiveness of God and his Church, and ask you for counsel, direction, and absolution.

Priest then pronounces this absolution. Another one may also be used.

Our Lord Jesus Christ, who offered himself to be sacrificed for us to the Father, and who conferred power on his Church to forgive sins, absolve you through my ministry by the grace of the Holy Spirit, and restore you in the perfect peace of the Church. *Amen.*

The Priest adds

The Lord has put away your sins.

Penitent   **Thanks be to God.**

The Priest concludes

Go (or abide) in peace, and pray for me, a sinner.

I Timothy 1:15

Psalms

Psalms Explained

Psalms come from a collection of sacred songs or hymns from the Old Testament of the Bible. This Book of Psalms is also called the Psalter. The Book of Psalms contains 150 Psalms, and these psalms were the hymnbook of the ancient people of Israel.

In the Hebrew language, the psalms are poetry. But unlike English poems, these poems do not rhyme. Often they take an idea and present it first in one way, then in a slightly different way in the next line. The psalms in our Bible express all kinds of feelings, from great joy to deep anger. You can find psalms to express many different moods. This helps us to remember that God is our God even when we are sad or angry, or feeling like we have failed.

Psalms are written in the Prayer Book in numbered verses. They can be read silently or aloud, or sung. The Church may have all the people say or sing them together, or the choir may sing a verse then the people sing the next verse.

The following pages contain a few verses from four psalms.

Psalm 23

1   The Lord is my shepherd;
     I shall not be in want.

2   He makes me lie down in green pastures
     and leads me beside still waters.

3   He revives my soul
     and guides me along right pathways
     for his Name's sake.

4   Though I walk through the valley of the
     shadow of death,

I shall fear no evil;
for you are with me;
your rod and your staff, they comfort me.

5   You spread a table before me in the
presence of those
who trouble me;
you have anointed my head with oil,
and my cup is running over

6   Surely your goodness and mercy shall
follow me all the days of my life,
and I will dwell in the house of the Lord
forever.

Psalm 34

1   I will bless the Lord at all times;
his praise shall ever be in my mouth.

2   I will glory in the Lord;
let the humble hear and rejoice.

3   Proclaim with me the greatness of the
Lord;
let us exalt his Name together.

8   Taste and see that the Lord is good;
        happy are they who trust in him.

Psalm 36

5   Your love, O Lord, reaches to the
        heavens,
        and your faithfulness to the clouds.

6   Your righteousness is like the strong
        mountains,
        your justice like the great deep;
        you save both man and beast, O Lord.

7   How priceless is your love, O God!
        your people take refuge under the
        shadow of your wings.

8   They feast upon the abundance of your
        house;
        you give them drink from the river of your
        delights.

9   For with you is the well of life,
        and in your light we see light.

10   Continue your loving–kindness to those
who know you,
and your favor to those who are true of
heart.

Psalm 148

1   Hallelujah!
Praise the Lord from the heavens;
praise him in the heights.

2   Praise him, all you angels of his;
praise him all his host.

3   Praise him, sun and moon;
praise him all you shining stars.

4   Praise him, heaven of heavens,
and you waters above the heavens.

5   Let them praise the Name of the Lord,
for he commanded, and they were
created.

6   He made them stand fast forever and ever;
he gave them a law which shall not pass
away.

7   Praise the Lord from the earth,
         you sea–monsters and the deeps;

8   Fire and hail, snow and fog
         tempestuous wind, doing his will;

9   Mountains and hills,
         fruit trees and all cedars;

10   Wild beasts and all cattle,
         creeping things and winged birds;

11   Kings of the earth and all peoples,
         princes and rulers of the world;

12   Young men and maidens,
         old and young together.

13   Let them praise the Name of the Lord,
         for his Name is exalted,
         his splendor is over earth and heaven.

14   He has raised up strength for his people
         and praise for all his loyal servants,
         the children of Israel, a people who are near
         him.
         Hallelujah!

Jesus Loves Us and Shows Us How to Show Our Love in Return

Jesus tells us the best way to show our love is to keep the Greatest Commandments.

The first one is:

> **You must love God with all your heart, all your soul, and your entire mind above all other things.**

The second one is:

> **You must love your neighbor as yourself.**

Exodus 20:1–17

Jesus tells us to obey the Ten Commandments that God gave Moses and the people of Israel at Mount Sinai a long time ago.

The first four show us how to love God.

1. **To love and obey God and to bring others to know God;**

2. **To put nothing in the place of God;**

3. **To show God respect in thought, word, and deed;**

4. **And to set aside regular times for worship, prayer, and the study of God's ways.**

The last six show us how to love our neighbors.

5. **To love, honor, and help our parents and family; to honor those in authority, and to meet their just demands;**

6. **To show respect for the life God has given us; to work and pray for peace; to bear no malice, prejudice, or hatred in our hearts; and to be kind to all the creatures of God;**

7. **To use our bodily desires as God intended;**

8. **To be honest and fair in our dealings; to seek justice, freedom, and the necessities**

of life for all people; and to use our talents and possessions as ones who must answer for them to God;

9. To speak the truth, and not to mislead others by our silence;

10. To resist temptations to envy, greed, and jealousy; to rejoice in other people's gifts and graces; and to do our duty for the love of God, who has called us into fellowship with God.

When we keep the commandments, we live as God's children.

The Sermon on the Mount

Jesus gathered his disciples and followers on a mountainside. Jesus taught them guidelines to follow to live a good life that God would love. As good Christians we try to follow in Jesus' words of wisdom.   *Matthew 5:1–12*

Under each of Jesus' guidelines are prayers asking God for help in living in this way.

Blessed are the poor in spirit,
for theirs is the kingdom of Heaven.
Lord, teach us to give of our hearts and to those in need, and not to be selfish with our possessions or time we can give to others. *Amen.*

Blessed are they who mourn,
for they will be comforted.
Lord, whenever we are sad or injured, please help to open our hearts to receive your loving comfort. Help us comfort others in their time of need. *Amen.*

Blessed are the meek,
for they will inherit the earth.

Lord, please help us to be humble, to appreciate others' talents and gifts, let us not brag upon ourselves. You have created all that we are and all that we have on this earth. Serving you we will inherit what you have promised. *Amen.*

Blessed are they who hunger and thirst for righteousness,
for they will be filled.

Lord, help us to seek your holy will. Keep us away from sinful ways and let us guide others in your ways of holiness. *Amen.*

Blessed are the merciful,
for they will receive mercy.

Lord, give us the strength to be kind to others, if there is suffering let us comfort, if there is not clothing let us cloth, where we see loneliness lets us be a friend. *Amen.*

Blessed are the pure of heart,
for they will see God.

Lord, help us to always be kind in our hearts and body and keep us away from the temptation to sin against you and others. For we wish to fulfill our goal to see you in eternity. *Amen.*

Blessed are the peacemakers,
for they shall be called children of God.

Lord, give us strength when we are challenged with a decision for peace. At home with our families or in school with our friends, help us to do what is right to be children of God. *Amen.*

Blessed are they who are persecuted for righteousness sake, for theirs is the kingdom of God.

Lord, help us to be faithful to your holy laws. With your help, we can reach your holy kingdom. *Amen.*

Prayers and Thanksgivings

Prayers for the World

For the Human Family

O God, you made us in your own image and redeemed us through Jesus your Son; Look with compassion on the whole human family; take away the arrogance and hatred which infect our hearts; break down the walls that separate us; unite us in bonds of love; and work through our struggle and confusion to accomplish your purposes on earth; that, in your good time, all nations and races may serve you in harmony around your heavenly throne; through Jesus Christ our Lord. *Amen.*

Almighty God our heavenly Father, guide the nations of the world into the way of justice and truth, and establish among them that peace which is the fruit of righteousness, that they may become the kingdom of our Lord and Savior Jesus Christ. *Amen.*

Prayers for the Church

Gracious Father, we pray for the holy Catholic Church. Fill it with all truth, in all truth with all peace. Where it is corrupt, purify it; where it is in error, direct it; where in anything it is amiss, and reform it. Where it is right, strengthen it; where it is in want, provide for it; where it is divided, reunite it; for the sake of Jesus Christ thy Son our Savior. *Amen.*

Ever living God, whose will it is that all should come to you through your Son Jesus Christ: Inspire our witness to him, that all may know the power of his forgiveness and the hope of his resurrection; who lives and reigns with you and the Holy Spirit, one God, now and forever. *Amen.*

Clergy and People

Almighty and everlasting God, by whose Spirit the whole body of your faithful people is governed and sanctified. Receive our supplications and our prayers, which we offer before you for all members of your holy Church, that in their vocation and ministry they may truly and devoutly serve you through our Lord and Savior Jesus Christ. *Amen.*

For the Parish

Almighty and everliving God, ruler of all things in heaven and earth, hear our prayers for this parish family. Strengthen the faithful, arouse the careless, and restore the penitent. Grant us all things necessary for our common life, and bring us all to be of one heart and mind within your holy Church; through Jesus Christ our Lord. *Amen.*

For those about to be baptized or to renew their Baptismal Covenant

O God, you prepared your disciples for the coming of the Spirit through the teaching of your Son Jesus Christ. Make the hearts and minds of your servants ready to receive the blessing of the Holy Spirit, that they may be filled with the strength of his presence; through Jesus Christ our Lord. *Amen.*

Father of all, we pray to you for those we love, but see no longer: Grant them your peace; let light perpetual shine upon them; and, in your loving wisdom and almighty power, work in them the good purpose of your perfect will; through Jesus Christ our Lord. *Amen*

O God, whom saints and angels delight to worship in heaven, be ever present with your servants who seek through art and music to perfect the praises offered by your people on earth. Grant to them even now glimpses of your beauty, and make them worthy at length to behold it unveiled forevermore; through Jesus Christ our Lord. *Amen.*

Prayers for National Life

For our Country

Almighty God, who has given us this good land for our heritage: We humbly ask you that we may always prove ourselves a people mindful of your favor and glad to do your will. Bless our land with honorable industry, sound learning, and pure manners. Save us from violence, discord, and confusion; from pride and arrogance, and from every evil way. Defend our liberties, and fashion into one united people the multitudes brought together out of many lands and languages. Give the spirit of wisdom to those whom in your Name we entrust the authority of government, that there may be justice and peace at home, and that, through obedience to your law, we may show forth your praise among the nations of the earth. In the time of prosperity, fill our hearts with thankfulness, and in the day of trouble, do not let our trust in you fail, all which we ask through Jesus Christ our Lord. *Amen.*

For those in the Armed Forces of our Country
Almighty God, we commend to your gracious care and keeping all the men and women of our armed forces at home and abroad. Defend them day by day with your heavenly grace; strengthen them in their trials and temptations; give them courage to face the perils which beset them; and grant them a sense of your abiding presence wherever they may be; through Jesus Christ our Lord. *Amen.*

Prayers for Social Order
In Times of Conflict
O God, you have bound us together in a common life. Help us, in the midst of our struggles for

justice and truth, to confront one another without hatred or bitterness, and to work together with mutual forbearance and respect; through Jesus Christ our Lord. *Amen.*

For Agriculture

Almighty God, we thank you for making the earth fruitful, so that it might produce what is needed for life: Bless those who work in the fields; give us seasonable weather; and grant that we may all share the fruits for the earth, rejoicing in your goodness; through Jesus Christ our Lord. *Amen.*

For the Unemployed

Heavenly Father, we remember before you those who suffer want and anxiety from lack of work. Guide the people of this land so to use our public and private wealth that all may find suitable and fulfilling employment, and receive just payment for their labor; through Jesus Christ our Lord. *Amen.*

For Schools and Colleges

O Eternal God, bless all schools, colleges, and universities [and especially _____,] that they may be lively centers for sound learning, new discovery, and the pursuit of wisdom; and grant that those who teach and those who learn may find you to be the source of all truth; through Jesus Christ our Lord. *Amen.*

Lord Christ, when you came among us, you proclaimed the kingdom of God in villages, towns, and lonely places: Grant that your presence and power may be known throughout this land. Have mercy upon all of us who live and work in rural areas [especially _____]; and grant that all the people of our nation may give thanks to you for food and drink and all other bodily necessities of life, respect those who labor to produce them, and honor the land and the water from which these good things come. All this we ask in your holy Name. *Amen.*

For the Poor and the Neglected

Almighty and most merciful God, we remember before you all poor and neglected persons whom it would be easy for us to forget: the homeless and the destitute, the old and the sick, and all who have none to care for them. Help us to heal those who are broken in body or spirit, and to turn their sorrow into joy. Grant this, Father, for the love of

your Son, who for our sake became poor, Jesus
Christ our Lord. *Amen.*

For the Oppressed
Look with pity, O heavenly Father, upon the
people in this land who live with injustice, terror,
disease, and death as their constant companions.
Have mercy upon us. Help us to eliminate our
cruelty to these our neighbors. Strengthen those
who spend their lives establishing equal protection
of the law
and equal opportunities for all. And grant that
every one of us may enjoy a fair portion of the
riches of this land; through Jesus Christ our Lord.
Amen.

For Stewardship of Creation
O merciful Creator, your hand is open wide to
satisfy the needs of every living creature: Make us
always thankful for your loving providence; and
grant that we, remembering the account that we
must one day give, may be faithful stewards of
your good gifts; through Jesus Christ our Lord,
who lives in reigns with you, in the unity of the
Holy Spirit, one God, now and forever. *Amen*

Prayers for Natural Order

For Knowledge of God's Creation

Almighty and everlasting God, you made the
universe with all its marvelous order, its atoms,
worlds, and galaxies, and the infinite complexity of
living creatures: Grant that, as we probe the
mysteries of your creation, we may come to know
you more truly, and more surely fulfill our role in
your eternal purpose; in the name of Jesus Christ
our Lord. *Amen.*

For the Conservation of Natural Resources

Almighty God, in giving us dominion over things
on earth, you made us fellow workers in your
creation: Give us wisdom and reverence so to use
the resources of nature, that no one may suffer
from our abuse of them, and that generations yet
to come may continue to praise you for your
bounty; through Jesus Christ our Lord. *Amen.*

For the Harvest of Lands and Waters

O, gracious Father, who open your hand and fills all
living things: Bless the lands and waters, and
multiply the harvests of the world; let your Spirit
go forth, that it may renew the face of the earth;
show your loving–kindness, that our land may give
increase; and save us from selfish use of what thou

give, that men and women everywhere may give you thanks; through Christ our Lord. *Amen.*

For the Future of the Human Race
O God our heavenly Father, you have blessed us and given us dominion over all the earth: Increase our reverence before the mystery of life; and give us new insight into your purposes for the human race, and new wisdom and determination in making provision for its future in accordance with your will; through Jesus Christ our Lord. *Amen.*

Prayers for Personal Life

For Those Who Live Alone

Almighty God, whose Son had nowhere to lay his head: Grant that those who live alone may not be lonely in their solitude, but that, following in his steps, they may find fulfillment in loving you and their neighbors; through Jesus Christ our Lord. *Amen.*

For the Aged

Look with mercy, O God our Father, on all whose increasing years bring them weakness, distress, or isolation. Provide for them homes of dignity and peace; give them understanding helpers, and the willingness to accept help; and, as their strength diminishes, increase their faith and their assurance of your love. This we ask in the name of Jesus Christ our Lord. *Amen.*

For a Birthday

O God, our times are in your hand: Look with favor, we pray, on you servant **N.**_____ as _____begins another year. Grant that _____ may grow in wisdom and grace, and strengthen _____trust in your goodness all the days of _____life; through Jesus Christ our Lord. *Amen.*

For Travelers

O God, our heavenly Father, whose glory fills the whole creation, and whose presence we find wherever we go: Preserve those who travel [in particular _____]; surround them with your loving care; protect them from every danger; and bring them in safety to their journey's end; through Jesus Christ our Lord. *Amen.*

For Guidance

Direct us, O Lord, in all our doings with *thy* most gracious favor, and further us with *thy* continual help; that in all our works begun, continued, and ended in *thee*, we may glorify *thy* holy Name, and finally, by *thy* mercy, obtain everlasting life; through Jesus Christ our Lord. *Amen.*

Thanksgivings

A General Thanksgiving

Accept, O Lord, our thanks and praise for all that you have done for us. We thank you for the splendor of the whole creation, for the beauty of this world, for the wonder of life, and for the mystery of love.

We thank you for the blessing of family and friends, and for the loving care which surrounds us on every side.

We thank you for setting us at tasks which demand our best efforts, and for leading us to accomplishments which satisfy and delight us.

We thank you also for those disappointments and failures that lead us to acknowledge our dependence on you alone.

Above all, we thank you for your Son Jesus Christ; for the truth of his Word and the example of his life; for his steadfast obedience, by which he

overcame temptation; for his dying, through which
he overcame death; and for his rising to life again,
in which we are raised to the life of your kingdom.
Grant us the gift of your Spirit, that we may know
him and make him known; and through him, at all
times and in all places, may give thanks to you in
all things. *Amen.*

Thanksgivings for the Church

For the Mission of the Church
Almighty God, you sent your Son Jesus Christ to
reconcile the world to yourself: We praise and
bless you for those whom you have sent in the
power of the Spirit to preach the Gospel to all
nations. We thank you that in all parts of the earth
a community of love has been gathered together
by their prayers and labors, and that in every place
your servants call upon your Name; for the
kingdom and the power and the glory are yours
forever. *Amen.*

For the Saints and Faithful Departed
We give thanks to you, O Lord our God, for all your
servants and witnesses of time past: for Abraham,
the father of believers, and Sarah his wife; for
Moses, the lawgiver, and Aaron, the priest; for

Miriam and Joshua, Deborah and Gideon, and Samuel with Hannah his mother; for Isaiah and all the prophets; for Mary, the mother of our Lord; for Peter and Paul and all the apostles; for Mary and Martha, and Mary Magdalene; for Stephen, the first martyr, and all the martyrs and saints in every age and in every land. In your mercy, O Lord our God, give us, as you gave to them, the hope of salvation and the promise of eternal life; through Jesus Christ our Lord, the first–born of many from the dead. *Amen.*

Thanksgiving for the Social Order

For the Diversity of Races and Cultures
O God, who created all peoples in your image, we thank you for the wonderful diversity of races and cultures in this world. Enrich our lives by ever–widening circles of fellowship, and show us your presence in those who differ most from us, until our knowledge of your love is made perfect in our love for all your children; through Jesus Christ our Lord. *Amen.*

Thanksgivings for the Natural Order

For the Beauty of the Earth

We give you thanks, most gracious God, for the beauty of earth and sky and sea; for the richness of mountains, plains, and rivers; for the songs of birds and the loveliness of flowers. We praise you for these good gifts, and pray that we may safeguard them for our posterity. Grant that we may continue to grow in our grateful enjoyment of your abundant creation, to the honor and glory of your Name, now and forever. *Amen.*

For the Harvest

Most gracious God, by whose knowledge the depths are broken up and the clouds drop down the dew: We yield thee hearty thanks and praise for the return of seed time and harvest, for the increase of the ground and the gathering in of its fruits, and for all other blessings of thy merciful providence bestowed upon this nation and people. And, we beseech thee, give us a just sense of these great mercies, such as may appear in our lives by a humble, holy, and obedient walking before thee all our days; through Jesus Christ our Lord, to whom, with thee and the Holy Ghost be all glory and honor, world without end. *Amen.*

Liturgical Church Seasons

The liturgical seasons are the way the Church marks time. There are seven seasons: Advent, Christmas, Epiphany, Lent, Holy Week, Easter and Pentecost.

1. Advent

At Church and at home we get ready to celebrate the Birth of our Lord Jesus. Lessons at our Church service and at Sunday school help us to prepare our hearts and homes for the coming of our Lord and Savior.

At many Churches, an Advent wreath is placed on a stand. The candles of the wreath represent the four weeks of Advent with the fifth candle symbolizing Christmas Day. There are four candles arranged around the wreath, three or four purple, sometimes one pink candle and a white one in the center. One candle is lighted each Sunday before Christmas. On Christmas the white candle is lighted. Many families also have Advent wreaths at home; they light a candle and say a special Advent prayer.

Isaiah 42:1–6, Luke 1:26 –38

2. Christmas

At our Church, we celebrate the Birth of our Lord with a special service. Many candles are lighted around the Church, the Christmas tree is all lighted, the priest gives us a special lesson about the coming of our Lord, incense is used, many Churches have a Christmas play with children, and throughout the service we join the choir in singing joyous Christmas carols.

Isaiah 9: 6–7, Luke 2: 1–20

3. Epiphany

Epiphany is the twelfth day after Christmas. We remember this to be the arrival of the three wise men or Magi at Bethlehem to welcome and see Our Lord Jesus. They brought him the gifts of gold, frankincense and myrrh. When the wise men looked into the face of Jesus it was revealed to them that they were truly looking into the face of the Son of God.

Isaiah 60: 1–6, 9, Matthew 2: 1–12

The Baptism of Our Lord

On the first Sunday after the epiphany we remember the baptism of our Lord Jesus in the

river Jordon and the Holy Spirit descending upon
him.
Isaiah 42: 1–9, Mark 1:1–11

Ordinary time

During this time we are called to remember
the life of Jesus. We recall the times with his family
Mary and Joseph, teaching his followers and
apostles, his many miracles, and the parables he
told people to teach them how to live better lives.
*Matthew 2: 13–23, Luke 2: 41–52, John 1:43, 2–11,
Mark 4: 35–41, Luke 9:10–17, Luke 10: 25–37, Luke
19 1–10*

4. Ash Wednesday

Marks the first day of Lent, during this time
we remember the forty days Jesus spent in the
desert praying and doing without food.

We attend the Ash Wednesday Church
service if we are able. At the service the priest rubs
ashes on our foreheads in the sign of the cross.
This reminds us we do not live forever.

Lent is five weeks, during this time we pray
to be kinder to our family our pets and our friends.
We try to do without something in our lives (as

Jesus did without food), and help others in any way we can.
Isaiah 58: 1–12

5. Palm Sunday

Palm Sunday begins Holy Week. We remember Jesus riding into Jerusalem on a donkey; the people welcomed Jesus by covering his path with palm branches and waving palms.

At Church, we are given palm leaf crosses and some palms to hold to remind us of this. At many Churches the people enter the Church holding the palms and singing a hymn of praise.
Mark 11: 1–9

Maundy Thursday

On this day, our Church remembers all of the events on the last day before the crucifixion of our Lord. We remember the betrayals Jesus endured, last supper, which is now our communion meal, and how Jesus served his friends by washing their feet.

Jesus prayed all night while the disciples slept. To recall this time, many people stay up all night praying. Some of them pray in front of the altar, where some of the Holy Sacrament of Jesus' body and blood is kept all night.

Matthew 26: 14 –28, John 13: 1–22

Good Friday

We remember Jesus' crucifixion, suffering, death and burial in the tomb. This day is called Good Friday because Jesus died for all our sins.

Some Churches use the Stations of the Cross for the Good Friday service. The Stations of the Cross move us through the last days of the life of Jesus. We stop at each Station to reflect and pray. There are fourteen Stations of the Cross.
Genesis 22: 1–18, John 18:1–40

Holy Saturday

We remember this day of Jesus' day of rest because this day was the Sabbath, the Holy Day of rest on which no work could be done. We usually use this time for quiet prayer.
Matthew 27: 57–66

6. Easter Day

Our Church celebrates the resurrection of our Lord Jesus Christ. We have a special service with a lesson about Jesus' return to life. The first Easter Service is a late night or very early morning one in which a big candle symbolizing new life is lit

from a fire outside and carried into the Church.
Lessons are then read, sometimes people are
baptized, and Holy Communion is celebrated. At
Easter we say and sing "Alleluia" for the first time
since Lent began.

People give each other symbols of new life
such as colored Easter eggs, marshmallow chicks
or chocolate bunnies.
Romans 6: 3–11, Matthew 28: 1–10

Ascension Day

Forty days after Jesus rose from the dead,
we remember He gave his disciples a
commandment and a promise. He commanded
them not to leave Jerusalem, and told them they
would receive the power of the Holy Spirit. Then
Jesus was lifted up and a cloud took him up to
heaven.
Acts 1: 1–11, Luke 24: 44–53

7. Pentecost

Fifty days after Jesus' Resurrection and ten
days after his Ascension to heaven, the disciples
were all gathered in a room. They were waiting for
Jesus' promise to be fulfilled. Then a strong gust of
wind filled the room, at that moment tongues of
flame began descending upon their heads. The

flames were of light; the flames did not burn the disciples. All of a sudden, each of them had the gift to speak in many different languages. They all could speak the good deeds of God to everyone.
Acts 2: 1–11

About Our Faith

About us as Humans

We are part of God's creation, made in the image of God.

We are created in the image of God, and God gave us free will to make choices: to love, to create, to reason, and to live in harmony with creation and with God.

When we make wrong choices, God can help us. We pray and ask for forgiveness. We try our best to make up for our wrongs.

God the Father

There is one God, the Father Almighty, creator of heaven and earth, of all that is, seen and unseen.

God created a beautiful universe. We are called to enjoy it and to take good care of it.

We are all created in God's image, and this means that all people are worthy of respect and honor. This shows God love and respect for creating us.

The Old Covenant

The Old Covenant is an agreement and promise God gave to the Hebrew people.

God promised that they would be his people to bring all the nations of the world to him.

In return as part of the Covenant between God and his people, God required that the people be faithful, love justice, show mercy to others, and to always love God above all else.

The covenant with the Hebrew people is to be found in the books that we call the Old Testament.

God's will for us is shown most clearly in the Ten Commandments.

Sin and Redemption

Sin is saying or doing things we know to be against God's will. Redemption is the act of God, which sets us free from the power of sin.

God sent the prophets to show us our need for redemption, and to announce the coming of the Messiah.

The Messiah is one sent by God to free us from the power of sin, so that with the help of God we may live in harmony with God, within ourselves, with our neighbors, and with all creation. The Messiah, or Christ, is Jesus of Nazareth, the only Son of God.

God the Son

Jesus is the only perfect image of the Father, and shows us the nature of God.
The nature of God revealed in Jesus is that God is love.

The divine Son became human, so that in him human beings might be adopted as children of God, and be made heirs of God's kingdom.

By his suffering and death, Jesus made the offering that we could not make; in him we are freed from the power of sin and reconciled or brought back in peace together with God.

We share in his victory over sin, suffering, and death when we are baptized into the New Covenant and become living members of Christ.

The New Covenant

The New Covenant is the new relationship with God given by Jesus Christ, the Messiah, to the apostles; and, through them, to all who believe in him.
In the New Covenant Christ promised to bring us into the kingdom of God and give life in all its fullness.

In return as part of the covenant between Christ and us, Christ wanted us to believe in him and keep his commandments.

The commandments taught by Christ are as follows.

You shall love the Lord your God with all your heart, with all your soul, and with your entire mind. This is the first and great commandment. The second commandment states that you shall love your neighbor as yourself.

What Christians believe about Christ is found in the Scriptures and summed up in the creeds.

The Creeds

The creeds are statements of our basic beliefs about God.

This Church uses two creeds: The Apostles' Creed and the Nicene Creed.

The Apostles' Creed is the ancient creed of Baptism; it is used in the Church's daily worship to recall our Baptismal Covenant.

The Nicene Creed is the creed of the universal Church, and is used at the Eucharist.

The Trinity

The Trinity is one God: Father, Son, and Holy Spirit.

The Father

God the Father is the Creator of the world and everything that is in it.

The Son

God the Son, Jesus, came down to live as a human in order to fix the relationship between all creation and God the Father.

The Holy Spirit

The Holy Spirit is the Third Person of the Trinity, God at work in the world and in the Church even now.

The Holy Spirit is revealed in the Old Covenant as the giver of life, the One who spoke through the prophets.

The Holy Spirit is revealed in the New Covenant as the Lord who leads us into all truth and enables us to grow in the likeness of Christ.

We recognize the presence of the Holy Spirit when we confess Jesus Christ as Lord and are brought into love and harmony with God, with ourselves, with our neighbors, and with all creation.

The Holy Scriptures

The Holy Scriptures, commonly called the Bible, are the books of the Old and New Testaments.

The Old Testament consists of books written by the people of the Old Covenant, under the inspiration of the Holy Spirit, to show God at work in nature and history.

The New Testament consists of books written by the people of the New Covenant, under the inspiration of the Holy Spirit, to set forth the life and teachings of Jesus and to proclaim the Good News of the Kingdom for all people.

The Church

The Church is the community of the New Covenant.

The Church is described in the Bible as the Body of which Jesus Christ is the Head and of which all baptized persons are members. It is called the People of God, the New Israel, a holy nation, a royal priesthood, and the pillar and ground of truth.

The Church is described in the creeds as one, holy, catholic, and apostolic.

The Church is one, because it is one Body, under one Head, our Lord Jesus Christ.

The Church is holy, because the Holy Spirit dwells in it, consecrates its members, and guides them to do God's work.

The Church is catholic, because it proclaims the whole Faith to all people, to the end of time.

The Church is apostolic, because it continues in the teaching and fellowship of the apostles and is sent to carry out Christ's mission to all people.

The mission of the Church is to restore all people to unity with God and each other in Christ.

The Church pursues its mission as it prays and worships, proclaims the Gospel, and promotes justice, peace, and love.

The Church carries out its mission through the ministry of all its members.

The Ministry

Every baptized person, adult or child, is a Minister of Christ's Church.

The duty of all Christians is to follow Christ; to come together week by week for corporate worship; and to work, pray, and pray for the spread of the kingdom of God.

Prayer and Worship

Prayer is responding to God, by thought and by deeds, with or without words.

Our Lord gave us the example of prayer known as the Lord's Prayer. The principle kinds of prayer are adoration, praise, thanksgiving, penitence, oblation, intercession, and petition.

Adoration is the lifting up of the heart and mind to God, asking nothing but to enjoy God's presence.

We praise God, not to obtain anything, but because God's Being draws praise from us.

Thanksgiving is offered to God for all the blessings of this life, for our redemption, and for whatever draws us closer to God.

In penitence, we confess our sins and make restitution where possible, with the intention to amend our lives.

Oblation is an offering of us, our lives and labors, in union with Christ, for the purposes of God.

Intercession brings before god the needs of others; in petition, we present our own needs, and that God's will may be done.

In corporate worship, we unite ourselves with others to acknowledge the holiness of God, to hear God's Word, to offer prayer, and to celebrate the sacraments.

The Sacraments

The seven sacraments are outward and visible signs of inward and spiritual grace, given by Christ as sure and certain means by which we receive that grace.
Grace is God's favor toward us, unearned and undeserved; by grace God forgives our sins, enlightens our minds, stirs our hearts, and strengthens our wills.

The two great sacraments given by Christ to his Church are Holy Baptism and the Holy Eucharist.

Holy Baptism

Holy Baptism is the sacrament by which God adopts us as his children and makes us members of Christ's Body, the Church, and inheritors of the kingdom of God.

The outward and visible sign in Baptism is water, in which the person is baptized in the Name of the Father, and of the Son, and of the Holy Spirit.

The inward and spiritual grace in Baptism is union with Christ in his death and resurrection, birth into God's family the Church, forgiveness of sins, and new life in the Holy Spirit.

At Baptism it is required that we renounce Satan, repent of our sins, and accept Jesus as our Lord and Savior.

Infants are baptized so that they can share citizenship in the Covenant, membership in Christ, and redemption by God.

Promises are made for them by their parents and sponsors, who guarantee that the infants will be brought up within the Church, to know Christ and be able to follow him.

The Holy Eucharist

The Holy Eucharist is the sacrament commanded by Christ for the continual remembrance of his life, death, and resurrection, until his coming again.

The Eucharist is called a sacrifice because the Church's sacrifice of praise and thanksgiving is the way by which the sacrifice of Christ is made present, and in which he unites us to his one offering of himself.

The Holy Eucharist is known by other names such as the Lord's Supper, and Holy Communion; it is also known as the Divine Liturgy, the Mass, and the Great Offering.

The outward and visible sign in the Eucharist is bread and wine, give and received according to Christ's command.

The inward and spiritual grace in the Holy Communion is the Body and Blood of Christ given to his people, and received by faith.

The benefits we receive in the Lord's Supper are the forgiveness of our sins, the strengthening of our union with Christ and one another, and the foretaste of the heavenly banquet which is our nourishment in eternal life.

When we come to the Eucharist it is required that we should examine our lives, repent of our sins, and be in love and charity with all people.

Other Sacramental Rites

Other Sacramental rites are confirmation, ordination, holy matrimony, reconciliation of a penitent, and unction.

They are different from the two Sacraments of Baptism and the Holy Eucharist because although they are means of grace, they are not necessary for all persons to receive.

Confirmation is the rite in which we express a mature commitment to Christ, and receive strength from the Holy Spirit through prayer and the laying on of hands by a bishop.

It is required of those to be confirmed that they have been baptized, are sufficiently instructed in the Christian Faith, are penitent for their sins, and are ready to affirm their confession of Jesus Christ as Savior and Lord.

Ordination is the rite in which God gives authority and the grace of the Holy Spirit to those being made bishops, priests, and deacons, through prayer and the laying on of hands by bishops.

Holy Matrimony is Christian marriage, in which the woman and man enter into a life–long union, make their vows before God and the Church, and receive the grace and blessing of God to help them fulfill their vows.

Reconciliation of a Penitent, or Penance, is the rite in which those who repent of their sins may confess them to God in the presence of a priest, and receive the assurance of pardon and the grace of absolution.

Unction is the rite of anointing the sick with oil, or the laying on of hands, by which God's grace is given for the healing of spirit, mind, and body.

The Christian Hope

The Christian hope is to live with confidence in newness and fullness of life, and to await the coming of Christ in glory, and the completion of God's purpose for the world.

By the coming of Christ in glory, we mean that Christ will come, not in weakness but in power, and will make all things new.

We pray for the dead, because we still hold them in our love, and because we trust that in God's presence those who have chosen to serve him will grow in his love, until they see him as he is.

We believe that Christ will come in glory and judge the living and the dead.

Our assurance as Christians is that nothing, not even death, shall separate us from the love of God, which is in Christ Jesus our Lord. *Amen.*

Glossary

Here, you will find words used in your book and in your Church.

–A–

Absolution – is the receiving of God's forgiveness, after confessing a Sin, by a priest or bishop.

Acolyte – is a person who carries a candle or a torch in procession at a Church service.

Advent – begins in the four weeks leading up to Christmas, and starts the Church Year; preparation time for the coming of Christ.

Advent Wreath – The Advent wreath is placed on a stand at many Churches and also sometimes in a special place in homes. It is made of greens with three or four purple candles, sometimes one pink candle and a white one in the center. The candles remind us of the four Sundays before Christmas. Each Sunday before Christmas a candle is lighted and a special Advent prayer is said. On Christmas the white candle in the center is lighted.

Alb – is a long, sleeved white linen vestment worn over the cassock (covering the body from neck to ankles).

Alleluia – meaning praise and joy, used in various parts of the liturgy, except during Lent. The word Alleluia is derived from the Hebrew, meaning, "Praise the Lord."

Alms – are the gifts of money or food to the poor or to those in need.

Alms Basin – is a large bowl or plate into which the people place money offerings.

Altar – the table of the Lord, where the Holy Eucharist is celebrated. The altar is at the front of most Churches and can be made from marble, granite or wood.

Altar Book – is the large book for the celebrant to use during the Church service. The Altar Book contains Texts from The Book of Common Prayer, liturgies and music.

Altar Cloth – the long fine white cloth used to cover the altar.

Altar Cross – A crucifix or cross that is on or around the altar.

Ambo – The podium where the lesson, sermon, and occasionally the Gospel are read.

Amen – Response that shows agreement at the end of a prayer, hymn, or anthem.

Ancestor – a relative of someone from the past.

Anglican – church in common with the Church of England.

Apostle – a messenger and follower. Jesus' twelve apostles were Simon (renamed by Jesus as Peter), Andrew, James, John, Philip, Bartholomew, Thomas, Mathew, James, Thaddeus, Simon the Zealot, Judas Iscariot, and Matthias.

Aspergillum – used for sprinkling holy water.

Archbishop of Canterbury – the lead bishop of the Church of England

Archbishop – a bishop who presides over a group of dioceses or a national Church.

Ascension – a feast which signifies the Ascension of our Lord Jesus Christ to glory.

Ash Wednesday – the day marking the beginning of Lent, a period of spiritual discipline.

Aumbry– where the Blessed Sacrament of Christ's Body and Blood are kept.

– B –

Baptism – the sacrament by which God adopts us as his children and makes us members of Christ's Body, the Church, and inheritors of the Kingdom of God.

Baptismal Font – where the sacrament of Holy Baptism is given.

Baptismal Water – the water blessed by a bishop or priest for use during Baptism.

Bible – the sacred book of Christianity containing the writings of the Old Testament and New Testament.

Bishop – lead pastor of a diocese.

Blessed Sacrament – The consecrated bread and wine (the Body and Blood of our Lord Jesus Christ) given during Eucharist.

Blessing – Bestowal of God's favor.

– C –

Cathedral – the official Church of a bishop of a diocese.

Catholic – means "universal." The Episcopal Church is a Catholic Church.

Celebrant – the bishop or priest.

Chalice – the cup into which the wine for the Eucharist is poured.

Christmas – a day celebrating the birth of Christ on December 25th. The Christmas season extends through the Feast of the Epiphany on January 6th.

Church Community – People who are united by a common religion.

Ciborium – A covered bowl in which the Blessed Sacrament is kept.

Cincture – the rope worn with an alb.

Clergy – group of ordained ministers in a Church.

Colors, Liturgical – different colors are used for the various seasons of the Church Year.

> **Red** – during Pentecost, Feast of Martyrs, and Holy Week.
> **White** – during the Feast of our Lord, Feasts of the Saints who were not martyrs, and Feasts of the Blessed Virgin Mary.
> **Green** – on the Sundays of ordinary days of the Church Year.
> **Blue** – during penitential occasions, and sometimes during Advent.
> **Purple or Violet** – during penitential occasions, Lent, and sometimes Advent.
> **Black** – on Good Friday

Communion – Christian sacramental meal; also known as the Eucharist

Confirmation – an affirmation of the faith and one's commitment to fulfilling the responsibilities of their Baptismal vows.

Congregation – the group of people present for the worship service.

Consecrate – to make into the Body or Blood of Christ.

Crucifer – a person who bears the cross in a religious procession.

Crucifix – a Christian symbol of the cross in many Churches with an image of the body of Christ on it.

Custom – a way of doing things that has become a common standard.

Cruets – Containers for the wine and water used at the Eucharist

– D –

Deacon – an ordained minister whose title means "servant".

Disciple – a follower of a teacher, like Jesus' disciples

Dismissal – the words which the deacon or celebrant says at the end of the Eucharist.

Divine – to be sacred or holy.

– E –

Easter – The time celebrating the Lord's resurrection.

Epiphany – the manifestation of Our Lord Jesus Christ observed on January 6th.

Episcopal – a Christian denomination in common with the Anglican Church and the Church of England.

Epistle – a reading of a letter from the New Testament at the Eucharist preceding the Gospel.

Eucharist – the main act of worship on Sundays and other occasions; the sacrament of the Holy Communion.

– F –

Faith – strong belief in the religion, and in God. To believe without proof.

Fifty Days of Easter – Starts on the Great Vigil of Easter and ends on the Day of Pentecost.

Flagon – large pitcher often used for wine at the Eucharist.

– G –

Gifts – the offerings of Bread and Wine presented to the celebrant.

Good Friday – the day on which the Crucifixion of Christ is remembered.

Gospel – the final lesson of the Word of God read by the deacon or priest. Readings from Matthew, Mark, Luke, or John.

Gospel Book – contains the Gospel lessons that are used at the Eucharist. The Gospels are found in the New Testament.

– *H* –

Holy Communion – the sacrament Jesus established for us during the Passover meal; the receiving of the Body and Blood of Christ.

Holy Saturday – a day commemorating the day that Jesus' body was laid to rest.

Holy Water – water blessed by a bishop or priest for use in blessing the people.

Host – the consecrated bread in the Eucharist.

Hymns – sacred words sung during the liturgy.

– *I* –

Incense – a fragrant powder burned in the coals of the thurible, used on special occasion.

– *L* –

Laity – all members of the Church, excluding the clergy.

Lectionary – contains Bible readings in the Episcopal Church daily throughout the Church Year.

Lector – someone who reads a lesson at the liturgy.

Lent – a period of forty days of penitence and preparation for Holy Week and Easter.

Lesson – any reading from the Bible except the Gospels or Psalms.

Liturgy – the entire worship service.

Lord's Supper – celebration of the Holy Eucharist. (See Holy Communion)

– M –

Maundy Thursday – the day on which the first Lord's Supper is celebrated.

Magi – the three wise men that brought gifts to Christ as a child.

Messiah – Jesus Christ; The King of the Jews; "The Anointed One."

– N –

Narthex – enclosed area at the entry of the nave of a Church.

Nave – where the congregation gathers for the liturgy; the main Church.

– O –

Oblations – the offerings to God at the Eucharist.

Oil – the liquid blessed by a bishop or priest, used for baptisms, Anointing the sick, and Anointing people in preparation for Baptism.

Ordination – the ritual that makes somebody a bishop, priest, or deacon.

– P –

Palm Sunday – the Sunday before Easter in which members of the congregation may carry blessed palms in a procession.

Paschal Candle – a large white candle which burns for all the services during the Fifty Days of Easter, and occasionally for baptisms and funerals.

Passion Week – Holy Week.

Passover –a Jewish festival remembering the escape of the Jews from Egypt, also known as the Exodus.

Paten – a plate on which the bread for the Eucharist is placed.

Pentecost, Day of – the remembrance of the descent of the Holy Spirit upon the disciples.

Pentecost, Season of – the time after the Day of Pentecost that ends on the Saturday before the First Sunday of Advent.

Pilgrimage – journey to a sacred place.

Priest – a person ordained by the Church who is responsible for performing Rites, preaching, administering sacraments, and giving blessings.

Procession – the line clergy, choir, acolytes, and others who walk into the Church to begin a service.

Proper – the readings and Collect appointed for the day or occasion.

Prophets – the holy men and women who passed on messages from God. Isaiah was one of the prophets in the Bible.

Psalm – sacred song or poem of praise that comes from the ancient Jewish hymn book.

– R –

Reader – someone who reads a lesson, psalm, or prayer in a service.

Resurrection – to be raised from the dead.

Reverence – a genuflection or solemn bow.

– S –

Saint – a saint is somebody who has died and gone to heaven. The Church officially recognizes certain people as saints for their religious deeds or experiences.

Sanctify – To consecrate, to make holy.

Scripture – The word of God found in the Old and New Testaments of the Bible.

Sermon – a talk, based on a Bible reading, that interprets the scripture and gives religious encouragement.

Sign of the Cross – The tracing of the sign of the cross on one's forehead, chest and shoulders.

– *T* –

Torch – a candle on a pole that an acolyte carries at the beginning of the service, during the Gospel Procession, and at the end of the service.

Twelve Days of Christmas – a period that lasts from Christmas on December 25th until the Epiphany on January 6th.

– *U* –

Unction – the rite of Anointing the sick with oil by which God's grace is given for the healing of spirit, mind, and body.

– *V* –

Vessels, Sacred – includes the Chalice, Paten, Ciborium, and Flagon.

Vestments – clothing worn by the Clergy.

Vigil – a period of preparation before a major celebration.

– W –

Wafer –an unleavened, thin, circular cracker symbolizing the Body of Christ; the Holy Host received during Holy Communion.

Way of the Cross – The Stations of the Cross move us through the last days of the life of Jesus. We stop at each Station to reflect and pray. There are fourteen Stations of the Cross:
1. He is condemned to death.
2. He carries His cross.
3. He falls.
4. Jesus meets His afflicted mother.
5. Simon helps carry Jesus' cross.
6. Veronica wipes His face.
7. Jesus falls again.
8. He meets the women of Jerusalem.
9. He falls a third time.
10. Jesus is stripped.
11. He is nailed to the cross.
12. He dies.
13. Jesus' body is taken down.

14. Jesus is buried.

Wine – symbolizes the blood of Christ.

Worship – the expression of love and devotion to God through participation in rites, services, and prayer.

Made in the USA
Coppell, TX
12 February 2021

50193094R10074